Hot Cocoa Bombs Recipes For A Warm Drink

Creative and Amazing Hot Cocoa Bombs Ideas To Make

Copyright © 2021

All rights reserved.

DEDICATION

The author and publisher have provided this e-book to you for your personal use only. You may not make this e-book publicly available in any way. Copyright infringement is against the law. If you believe the copy of this e-book you are reading infringes on the author's copyright, please notify the publisher at: https://us.macmillan.com/piracy

Contents

WHAT IS A HOT CHOCOLATE BOMB? 1

TIKTOK'S VIRAL HOT CHOCOLATE BOMBS 3

PEPPERMINT HOT CHOCOLATE BOMB 12

WHITE HOT CHOCOLATE BOMBS 28

PEANUT BUTTER HOT CHOCOLATE BOMBS 36

GRINCH HOT CHOCOLATE BOMBS 47

What Is A Hot Chocolate Bomb?

Hot chocolate bombs are hollow, chocolate, sphere shells, filled with hot cocoa mix and lots of mini marshmallows. You can also add your favorite flavours to make hot chocolate.

So that's what the bomb is, what you do next with it is the fun part!!

You place the bomb into an empty mug and you pour hot milk over it.

The shell begins to melt away and the mini marshmallows all float to the top! Give your hot chocolate a quick stir and you have a warm and cozy cup of hot cocoa!

This is a really fun idea for kids and sharing with guests who come over for the holidays. You can also make them ahead of time and share them as gifts!

Tiktok's Viral Hot Chocolate Bombs

INGREDIENTS

There are only three must-have ingredients to make these hot chocolate bombs.

Chocolate – You can use milk, semi-sweet or dark, it's totally up to you. Chocolate chips work fine, just choose a higher quality brand. You can also use good quality chocolate bars or baking chocolate.

Cocoa mix – Use your favourite here. The better quality brand you choose the tastier your hot chocolate will be.

Marshmallows – Mini marshmallows will work best. If you like the coloured marshmallows you can use those, or stick with the traditional ones.

You will probably want to decorate your cocoa bombs as well. I like to use a variety of fun sprinkles, but you can use crushed mints, shaved chocolate, or a simple drizzle of white chocolate. Get creative and have fun!

Hot Cocoa Bombs Recipes For A Warm Drink

INSTRUCTIONS

One – Melt the chocolate. I prefer to do this in a glass bowl over a simmering pot of water. I have better control of the melting than using a microwave and I can keep the bowl over the hot water as I work which keeps it the perfect consistency.

Fill the pot just full enough so the bottom of the bowl just barely touches the water. Heat over medium-low heat (I use setting 4 on my stove-top) until melted and smooth.

Remove the pot from the heat leaving the bowl in place.

Two – Spoon about 2 teaspoons of chocolate into each mold.

Expert Tip – If you are going to use the microwave to heat your chocolate do so slowly. Use 15 second intervals and stir between each interval. Once the chocolate is mostly melted you should be able to stir it well enough to melt the rest. If it still needs a bit longer, reduce to 5 second intervals to avoid burning the chocolate.

Three – Using a pastry brush, brush the chocolate over the inside of the mold as evenly as you can making sure to spread it right to the top.

Four – Once all the molds are filled, pop the tray in the freezer for 5-10 minutes so the chocolate can firm up. Then repeat the filling, brushing and freezing one more time.

On the second coat of chocolate fill and brush one mold at a time otherwise the cold chocolate will set the melted chocolate before you can spread it.

Five – Remove the molds from the freezer. Loosen the chocolate by gently stretching the edges of the molds.

Fill 6 halves with cocoa mix and marshmallows. I have found 1 tablespoon of mix and 5-6 marshmallows are perfect.

Hot Cocoa Bombs Recipes For A Warm Drink

Six – Place a clean plate over the hot pot of water. The steam will warm the plate.

Remove the empty halves from the mold and, working one at a time, press the edge of the chocolate shell to the warm plate.

Seven – When you see the edge start to melt remove it from the plate and press it to a filled half. Hold it for 2-3 seconds to seal. Then repeat with remaining shells.

Once all the bombs are sealed, pop them in the freezer for a couple minutes so the edges will set.

I tried many ways to seal the halves together and found this was the easiest and most successful way of doing it. You could also place some melted chocolate in a piping bag with a fine tip and pipe melted chocolate around the edge of the empty half and then press it to the filled half.

Remove from the freezer, and carefully pop the hot chocolate bombs out of the molds.

Decorate with a drizzle of melted chocolate and sprinkles or any way you like.

If you want to make these extra special, try making your own marshmallows! It isn't as hard as you'd think.

Peppermint Hot Chocolate Bomb

What You Need to Make

Chocolate Sphere Mold – You can use a truffle size but 2 inches and larger is ideal for filling and yields the most amazing cup of hot chocolate. I prefer a 2.5 inch mold. It's the perfect amount of chocolate for 1 cup of hot milk (or water).

Baking Sheet – Any will do! It makes transferring them to and from the refrigerator or freezer easy, and makes a great surface to drip out the excess chocolate.

Peppermint Hot Chocolate Bomb Ingredients

Chocolate – Milk chocolate melting wafers are my go-to for luxuriously silky chocolate, but chocolate chips and baking chocolate will also work. I experimented with both white chocolate and milk chocolate for this recipe and both worked beautifully.

Mini Marshmallows – Traditional work as well, but you can't pack too many into the bomb. You can also use the freeze dried marshmallows (the type that come inside boxes of cereal).

Hot Chocolate Mix – Store-bought or homemade. It's so easy to make your own (eliminate dry milk)!

Crushed Peppermint – This gives you the burst of peppermint flavor! You can purchase crushed peppermint or crush your own using mallet. Candy canes are easier to crush. Simply place in a plastic bag (for easy cleanup) and run a rolling pin over it.

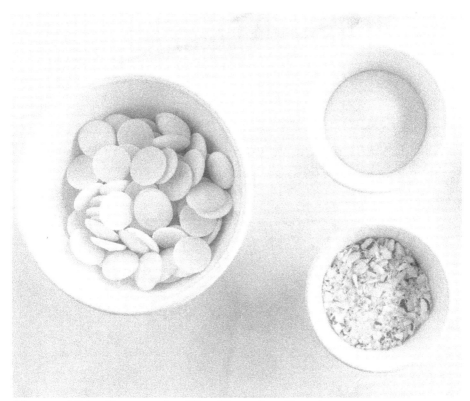

How to Make Peppermint Hot Chocolate Bombs

Melt Chocolate – To begin, melt chocolate in a small, microwave-safe bowl on 50% power in 15 second increments, stirring in between, until smooth or milk chocolate on regular power in 15 second increments, stirring in between, until smooth.

Fill Mold – Next, add a heaping spoonful of melted chocolate to each cavity. Using the back of a teaspoon, spread until completely covered.

Eliminate Excess – Invert mold onto a parchment lined baking sheet and lightly shake to remove excess. Discard parchment and place mold on baking sheet (chocolate side up). Scrape edges of each cavity if needed.

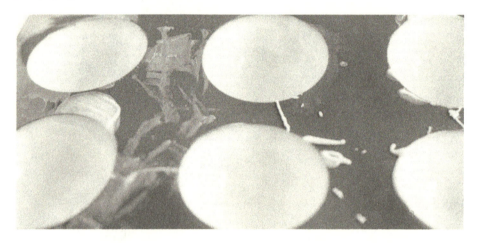

Freeze to Set – Freeze 7 minutes.

Warm Plate and Spoon – Meanwhile warm a plate in the microwave, dishwasher or oven and boil a glass of water to warm a spoon.

Remove – Remove mold from freezer. Flip over and press gentlly on the top of each sphere to carefully onto your baking sheet.

Fill – Remove from freezer and fill each of 3 spheres with a tablespoon of white hot chocolate mix, 1 tablespoon crushed peppermint, 2 tablespoons marshmallow bits.

Seal – Place the bottom of an empty sphere on the hot plate to lightly melt chocolate. Place the melted chocolate edge on filled half to seal, handling the chocolate as little as possible. Optional: If needed, dip a spoon in hot water, dry and run the back of it along the edges to seal.

Decorate – Decorate using melted chocolate in a piping or sealable bag with the tip clipped and quickly top with crushed peppermint

Set – To fully set, freeze five minutes or refrigerate 30 minutes and store at room temperature until ready to serve.

How to Use a Peppermint Hot Chocolate Bomb

To make a cup of hot chocolate, place one peppermint hot chocolate bomb in a mug.

Pour one cup of hot milk over bomb.

Stir until incorporated and enjoy!

Hot Cocoa Bombs Recipes For A Warm Drink

Serving Suggestions

Top with homemade whipped cream

Garnish with more crushed peppermint

Serve and stir with a candy cane

A clear glass mug of peppermint hot chocolate, topped with tiny marshmallows and crushed peppermint.

Gifting Suggestions

These clear glass mugs are the perfect diameter for this size of hot chocolate bomb. Bonus! It's so much fun to watch the melting happen before your eyes. You can wrap Hot Chocolate Bombs in mugs with cellophane and tie with a ribbon for gifting!

Or you can wrap individually in cellophane bags and seal with a personalized label or piece of washi tape.

Tips

Read Instructions Thoroughly Before Starting – It's actually so quick that it's best to read the recipe first and be prepared.

Don't Overheat – White chocolate can burn. To prevent burning, stir every 15 seconds until smooth.

Touch Minimally – Chocolate warms quickly. Touch as minimally as possible to prevent spheres from changing shape or making fingerprints.

Adjust Serving Size – Want to double or triple this recipe? Use the 1x2x3x tab in the printable recipe to change the calculations for you!

Is it better to make hot chocolate with milk or water?

You can use either! We prefer to use milk because it creates a creamier experience. However, water can allow the characteristics of your chocolate to shine, so it's totally a personal preference!

What's good to put in hot chocolate?

All the sweet additions! Marshmallows and whipped cream are classic hot chocolate toppers, but you can also add liquor like Peppermint Schnapps!

A clear glass mug of peppermint hot chocolate, topped with tiny marshmallows and crushed peppermint.

How to Store

Room Temperature – Store at room temperature for up to two weeks in an airtight container or a food safe cellophane bag. Store in a dark pantry.

Refrigerator – Peppermint hot chocolate bombs can be temporarily refrigerated, but will cause condensation.

A white chocolate hot chocolate bomb topped with crushed peppermint on a marble surface.

A white chocolate hot chocolate bomb topped with crushed peppermint on a marble surface.

A clear glass mug of peppermint hot chocolate, topped with tiny marshmallows and crushed peppermint.

White Hot Chocolate Bombs

These white chocolate hot chocolate bombs are the cutest way to make a sweet, creamy and steamy mug of white hot chocolate! These white hot chocolate bombs are perfect for holiday gifts, too.

White chocolate hot cocoa bombs are the best way to warm the hearts of friends and family this winter, and they are so easy to make!

What You need to Make Chocolate Bombs

Chocolate Sphere Mold – You can use a truffle size but 2 inches and larger is ideal for filling and yields the most amazing cup of hot chocolate. I prefer a 2.5 inch mold. It's the perfect amount of chocolate for 1 cup of hot milk

Clear Glass Mugs – These are the perfect diameter for this size of hot chocolate bomb. Bonus! It's so much fun to watch the melting happen before your eyes. You can wrap Hot Chocolate Bombs in mugs with cellophane and tie with a ribbon for gifting!

Baking Sheet – Any will do! It makes transferring them to and from the refrigerator or freezer easy, and makes a great surface to drip out the excess chocolate.

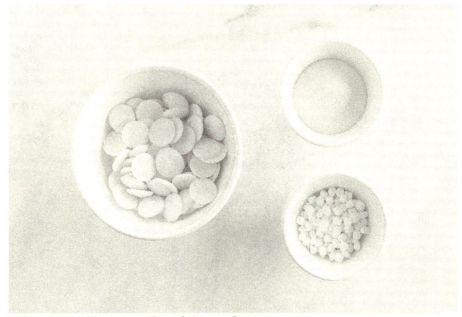

White Hot Chocolate Bomb Ingredients

White Chocolate – White melting wafers, chocolate chips or baking chocolate.

Marshmallow Bits – So fun to fill hot chocolate bombs and add to the creamy consistency.

White Hot Chocolate Mix – Store-bought or homemade white hot chocolate mix fills the bombs to add an extra dose of creamy white chocolate flavor.

A white plate with a white chocolate hot chocolate bomb topped in Christmas sprinkles.

How to Make White Hot Chocolate Bombs

Melt Chocolate – To begin, melt white chocolate in a small, microwave-safe bowl on 50% power in 15 second increments, stirring in between, until smooth.

Fill Mold – Next, add a heaping spoonful of melted chocolate to each cavity. Using the back of a teaspoon, spread until completely covered.

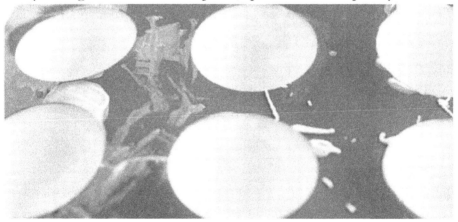

Eliminate Excess – Invert mold onto a parchment lined baking sheet and lightly shake to remove excess. Discard parchment and place mold on baking sheet (chocolate side up). Scrape edges of each cavity if needed.

Freeze to Set – Freeze 7 minutes. A gold baking tray with half spheres of white chocolate for hot chocolate bombs.

Remove mold from freezer. White chocolate side down, press gently on the top of each sphere to carefully remove onto your baking sheet.

Warm Plate and Spoon – Meanwhile warm a plate in the microwave, dishwasher or oven and boil a glass of water to warm a spoon.

Fill – Remove from freezer and fill each of 3 spheres with a tablespoon of white hot chocolate mix and 2 tablespoons marshmallow bits. A white chocolate hot cocoa bomb on a white plate, split in half to show marshmallows and mix.

Seal – Place the bottom of an empty sphere on the hot plate to lightly melt chocolate. Place the melted chocolate edge on filled half to seal, handling the chocolate as little as possible. Optional: If needed, dip a spoon in hot water, dry and run the back of it along the edges to seal.

Decorate – Decorate using melted chocolate in a piping or sealable bag with the tip clipped and quickly top with marshmallow bits, crushed peppermint or sprinkles.

Set – To fully set, freeze five minutes or refrigerate 30 minutes and store at room temperature until ready to serve.

White hot chocolate bombs on a marble surface.

How to Use a White Hot Chocolate Bomb

To make a cup of hot chocolate, place one white hot chocolate bomb in a mug.

Pour one cup of hot milk over bomb.

Stir until incorporated and enjoy!

Serving Suggestions

Top with homemade whipped cream

Garnish with crushed peppermint or white chocolate shavings

A white plate with a white chocolate hot chocolate bomb topped in Christmas sprinkles.

Tips

Read Instructions Thoroughly Before Starting – It's actually so quick that it's best to read the recipe first and be prepared.

Don't Overheat – White chocolate can burn, stir every 15 seconds until smooth.

Adjust Serving Size – Want to double or triple this recipe? Use the 1x2x3x tab in the printable recipe to change the calculations for you!

Do I need to temper my chocolate? And what does "temper" actually mean?

Tempering is the process of gradually raising and lowering the temperature of melted chocolate (constantly stirring as you do so). While many hot chocolate bomb recipes require perfectly tempered chocolate, this one does not! It's so easy!

How to Store

Room Temperature – Store at room temperature for up to two weeks in an airtight container or a food safe cellophane bag. Store in a dark pantry.

Refrigerator – Peppermint hot chocolate bombs can be temporarily refrigerated, but will cause condensation.

Peanut Butter Hot Chocolate Bombs

If you love a cozy, creamy mug of steaming hot chocolate, you're going to love these Peanut Butter Hot Chocolate Bombs. Enjoy the eternally delicious combination of creamy peanut butter and chocolate as the bomb melts in your mug!

Peanut butter and chocolate is the perfect pairing. It's sweet and salty and absolutely perfect for a cup of hot chocolate! This peanut butter hot chocolate bomb proves just how good that combo can be!

What You Need to Make Peanut Butter Hot Chocolate Bombs

Chocolate Sphere Mold – You can use a truffle size but 2 inches and larger is ideal for filling and yields the most amazing cup of hot chocolate.

Baking Sheet – Any will do! It makes transferring them to and from the refrigerator or freezer easy, and makes a great surface to drip out the excess chocolate.

Plate – A warm plate is the easiest way to gently melt the chocolate to seal your bombs.

Peanut Butter Hot Chocolate Bomb Ingredients

Ingredients

Chocolate melting wafers make this project super easy, but chocolate chips will work as well!

Hot Chocolate Mix – It's so easy to make your own!

Creamy Peanut Butter – Creamy is important because we don't want any chunks in our creamy mug of cocoa. You can use a traditional peanut butter, natural, or whatever you prefer.

Two peanut butter hot chocolate bombs on a marble surface, drizzled with peanut butter and white chocolate.

Variations

Make Cookie Butter Bombs – Simply substitute peanut butter with cookie butter!

How to Make Peanut Butter Hot Chocolate Bombs

Melt Chocolate – To begin, melt milk chocolate in a small, microwave-safe bowl in the microwave in 15 second increments, stirring each time, until smooth.

Fill Mold – Next, add a heaping spoonful of melted milk chocolate to each cavity. Using the back of a teaspoon, spread until completely covered.

Eliminate Excess – Invert chocolate mold onto a parchment lined baking sheet (for easy cleanup) and lightly shake to remove excess. Discard parchment and place mold on baking sheet (chocolate side up). Scrape edges of each cavity if needed.

Freeze to Set – Freeze chocolate bombs 7 minutes to set.

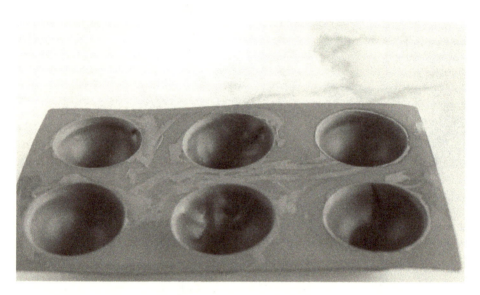

Warm Plate (and Spoon) – Meanwhile warm a plate in the microwave, dishwasher or oven and boil a glass of water to warm a spoon.

Remove – Remove mold from freezer. Flip mold over. Gently press on the top of each sphere to remove.

Hot Cocoa Bombs Recipes For A Warm Drink

1 tbsp peanut butter

Fill – Remove mold from freezer and fill 3 spheres with a tablespoon of hot chocolate mix and a tablespoon of creamy peanut butter.

Seal – Place the bottom of an empty sphere on the hot plate to lightly melt chocolate. Place the melted chocolate edge on filled half to seal, handling the chocolate as little as possible. Optional: If needed, dip a spoon in hot water, dry and run the back of it along the edges to seal.

Decorate – Decorate using melted peanut butter in a piping or sealable bag with the tip clipped and quickly move back and forth over each bomb.

Hot Cocoa Bombs Recipes For A Warm Drink

Set – To fully set, freeze five minutes or refrigerate 30 minutes and store at room temperature until ready to serve.

How to Use A Peanut Butter Hot Chocolate Bomb

To make a cup of peanut butter hot chocolate, place bomb in a mug.

Pour one cup of hot milk (or water) over bomb.

Stir until chocolate and peanut butter have melted and enjoy!

Serving Suggestions

Top with homemade whipped cream

Add marshmallows

Top with chocolate shavings

Garnish with a drizzle of warm peanut butter

Garnished with crushed chocolate or peanuts

A marble surface with a variety of hot chocolate bombs.

Tips

Read Instructions Before Starting – It's actually so quick that it's best to read the recipe first and be prepared.

Don't Overheat – Chocolate can burn, stir every 15 seconds until smooth.

Handle Chocolate Spheres Minimally – Chocolate softens easily. If you hold them or touch them you can leave fingerprints or alter their shape. Work quickly and touch them as minimally as possible for best results.

A mug of peanut butter hot chocolate with hot milk being poured in.

What kind of chocolate should I use for hot chocolate bombs?

Any kind of chocolate will work! Milk or dark chocolate chips, wafers or baking chocolate.

I don't have a silicone mold. What else can I use?

Try using muffin tins or any other type of mold you have on hand. They don't have to be a perfect sphere, so feel free to get creative!

Three peanut butter hot chocolate bombs, drizzled with peanut butter and white chocolate.

How to Store

Room Temperature – Store at room temperature for up to two weeks in an airtight container or a food safe cellophane bag. Store in a dark pantry.

Grinch Hot Chocolate Bombs

Grinch hot chocolate bombs make the cutest, most festive gift for the holiday season! Watching them melt into a creamy, dreamy mug of green hot chocolate is so much fun!

Just like the Grinch himself, you'll be all toasty inside when you try these cozy and adorable Grinch Hot Chocolate Bombs!

What You Need to Make Chocolate Bombs

Chocolate Sphere Mold – A 2.5 inch mold makes the perfect amount of chocolate for 1 cup of hot milk. 2 inches or larger will be ideal for filling with hot cocoa mix and marshmallows, and yields the most amazing cup of hot chocolate. You can use a truffle size in a pinch. A marble surface with a silicone sphere mold.

Clear Glass Mugs – Clear glass mugs make it easy to watch the grinch melt before your eyes! They are the perfect diameter for a hot chocolate bomb. You can even wrap these cute Hot Chocolate Bombs in mugs with cellophane and tie with a ribbon for an affordable and charming handmade gift!

Baking Sheet – Any will do! It makes transferring them to and from the refrigerator or freezer easy, and makes a great surface to drip out the excess chocolate.

What You Need to Make Grinch Hot Chocolate Bombs

White Chocolate – White chocolate melting wafers are my preference, but white chocolate chips and baking chocolate also work well.

Green Food Coloring – To make him green, of course!

Hot Chocolate Mix – White hot chocolate mix is preferred for a pretty green cup of cocoa.

Marshmallows – You can use miniature marshmallows as well.

Red Heart Sprinkles – If you don't have any red hearts, you can also use a red edible marker or red icing gel.

Optional – Black and yellow writing markers to draw the Grinch's face!

Variation

If you're not worried about controlling the color of your green chocolate sphere, try these bright green candy melts instead of white plus food coloring!

How to Make Grinch Hot Chocolate Bombs

Melt Chocolate – Melt white chocolate in a small, microwave-safe bowl on 50% power in 15 second increments, stirring in between, until smooth. Stir in green food coloring.

stir in green food coloring

Fill Mold – Add a large spoonful of melted white (green!) chocolate to each cavity. Using the back of the spoon, spread until completely covered.

Eliminate Excess – Invert mold onto a parchment lined baking sheet and lightly shake to remove excess. Discard parchment and place mold on baking sheet (green chocolate side up). Scrape edges of each cavity if needed.

Freeze to Set – Freeze 7 minutes or allow to set at room temperature.

Warm Plate and Spoon or Skillet – Meanwhile warm a plate in the microwave, dishwasher or oven or warm a skillet on low. Boil a glass of water to warm a spoon.

Fill – Remove chocolate from molds by gently pressing on the top of each sphere. Fill each of 3 spheres with a tablespoon of white hot chocolate mix, marshmallows and a red heart.

Seal – Place the bottom of an empty sphere on the hot plate to lightly melt chocolate. Place the melted chocolate edge on filled half to seal, handling the chocolate as little as possible. Optional: If needed, dip a spoon in hot water, dry and run the back of it along the edges to seal.

Decorate – Using leftover chocolate or writing icing, add a touch to the back of a heart and press onto the top of your chocolate mold. To make a grinch face, make two yellow circles for eyes, black eyebrows and mouth.

How to Use Grinch Hot Chocolate Bombs

Place the Grinch in a mug.

Pour one cup of hot milk over bomb. Watch as it turns green and reveals a heart two sizes too small.

Stir until incorporated and enjoy!

A green grinch hot chocolate bomb in a clear glass mug, a second bomb to the side on a marble surface.

"And what happened, then? Well, in Whoville they say – that the Grinch's small heart grew three sizes that day. And then – the true meaning of Christmas came through, and the Grinch found the strength of ten Grinches, plus two!"

Serving Suggestions

Top with homemade whipped cream

Serve and stir with a candy cane

Add extra marshmallows – because if some is good, more is better!

Top with crushed peppermint

Tips

Have all ingredients and materials ready. This recipe is so quick it's best to be prepared.

Careful not to burn the chocolate. Stir every 15 seconds until smooth.

How much do chocolate bombs cost?

While you can occasionally find them inexpensively in pre-packaged boxes at grocery stores, bakeries often charge $4-$8 per hot chocolate bomb!

Is it better to make hot chocolate with milk or water?

While you can certainly use water instead of milk, it won't create the same creamy results in both taste and feel.

You can see the heart in the bottom of the glass!

How to Store

Room Temperature – Store at room temperature for up to two weeks in an airtight container or a food safe cellophane bag. Store in a dark pantry.

CPSIA information can be obtained
at www.ICGtesting.com
Printed in the USA
LVHW091304081221
705631LV00018B/206